Original title:
Roots in Every Corner

Copyright © 2025 Creative Arts Management OÜ
All rights reserved.

Author: Helena Marchant
ISBN HARDBACK: 978-1-80581-839-7
ISBN PAPERBACK: 978-1-80581-366-8
ISBN EBOOK: 978-1-80581-839-7

Threads of Heritage

In a quirk of fate, uncle Steve
Dances like a chicken on Christmas Eve,
Grandma's stories, wild and grand,
A cat that plays the band!

In Every Cranny

Under the couch, old shoes reside,
Uncles sneak off to the rollercoaster ride,
A squirrel pilfering snacks from the chair,
We laugh till we cry; oh brother, beware!

The Depths We Know

A treasure map made by sight, not sound,
Where bologna sandwiches are riches profound,
Tales of adventure and questionable deeds,
Like finding a cousin who really just breeds!

Lifelines through Time

From telephones made of tin and string,
To TikToks that make our heads spin and cling,
Sharing secrets over cups of warm tea,
With laughter, we connect, you and me!

The Underground Symphony

In the depths, a band takes flight,
With moles on drums, they jam all night.
Rats play strings with nimble paws,
While rabbits sing, inspiring applause.

The concert's loud, the soil shakes,
As worms dance 'round with daring breaks.
The roots provide the finest stage,
For furry stars to earn their wage.

Paths Unseen

Through cracks and crevices we roam,
A secret world we call our home.
With ants as our tour guides, we tread,
On pathways that are seldom read.

A squirrel stops and shares its tale,
Of acorns lost in storms and hail.
Together, we laugh, we trip, we fall,
Finding treasures in the crawl.

Pillars of Memory

In compost heaps, our memories sleep,
Of summer days and secrets to keep.
A sunflower's dance, a wilting tale,
Of sneaky weeds that won the trail.

Laughter echoes from the vine,
As bunnies sip on dandelion wine.
Oh what a history, rich and vast,
With each notch, the moments last.

The Weaving of Legacy

A spider spins in whispered thread,
A tapestry of laughter spread.
With each design, new stories bloom,
In every stitch, a fateful tune.

The butterflies giggle in colorful show,
While grasshoppers hop in a rhythmic flow.
With nature's loom, we craft and play,
Creating joy in our own clay.

Where Shadows Meet the Light

In the garden, a gnome sits tight,
Hiding secrets, avoiding the light.
He drinks his tea with a tiny spoon,
Watches the flowers dance to a tune.

The squirrels chat, with a nutty plan,
Debating the best way to outsmart a man.
But little do they know, at dusk they'll see,
The cat in a hat, sipping chamomile tea.

Stories Buried in the Ground

Digging deep, I found a shoe,
A lost sandal, for a foot so blue.
It whispers tales of a beach day lost,
Where sandcastles fell, no matter the cost.

Beneath the surface, old toys lie,
A rubber chicken and a Frisbee high.
They giggle and squawk, reliving the fun,
While ants take a ride, under the sun.

Kinship of the Wilderness

A raccoon prances, wearing a cap,
He calls out to friends, 'Come join my nap!'
In a treehouse built from sparkling dreams,
They share tales of mischief and daredevil schemes.

The owl hoots loud, with a wink and a smile,
'You can't catch the breeze if you sit for a while!'
So the critters conspire under moonlit skies,
Laughing together as adventures arise.

Echoing Footsteps through the Ages

In a hallway lined with dusty shoes,
Ghosts of laughter, and ancient blues.
A slapstick skit from a time long past,
Where mischief and giggles forever last.

Old portraits whisper, with grins so wide,
'The fun never ends when you take it in stride!'
They tap dance together, in an echoing trance,
Offering the viewer a whimsical chance.

Hues of Heritage

In the attic, old hats stack high,
A feathered thing that makes me sigh.
Grandpa's shoes with a little squeak,
Just wait till they try to speak!

All those tales of yesteryears,
Made me giggle, brought out cheers.
A family photo, quite a sight,
Cousin Bob's dance moves, pure delight!

Dance of colors, like paint splashes,
Tales of laughter, oh how it thrashes.
Grandma's quilt, with threads so bright,
I wrapped it 'round, what a silly fright!

In every frame, a smile or two,
Extra chin? Well, that's the new you!
Heritage feels like a funny game,
Every layer, easy to blame!

The Embrace of Echoes

Echoes of laughter behind the wall,
A cat that thinks it knows it all.
Uncle Joe's jokes that flop and fall,
But we still give him the loudest call!

Chairs creaking like they have a tale,
While Aunt Sue serves up a giant snail.
We laugh till our sides go round and round,
In a circle of love, happily bound!

Voices of old, a funny replay,
"There's a ghost in the garden," they say.
But it's just the neighbor in green socks,
Trying to dance while he mows the blocks!

Round the fire, stories ignite,
"How did they meet?" Is that a fright?
Well, that's how the laughter grows wide,
In echoes, we take our fun-filled ride!

Legacy's Embrace

A cupboard of treasures, socks with holes,
They must be cherished, like ancient scrolls.
A faint smell of flour from Grandma's pie,
And a reminisce of who and why!

An heirloom spoon, a funny butler's dream,
"Beware!" it says, "I'll make you scream!"
Baked beans boogie, on granddad's plate,
A family feast that's truly first-rate!

Old letters tucked in a dusty crate,
"Dear cousin, you're just a little late!"
The more they call, the more we grin,
It's all a laugh, let the fun begin!

Legacy binds us with giggles and cheer,
In every memory, love stays near.
So come on over, there's fun to embrace,
In every tale, we find our place!

Journeys through Hidden Places

In a park where grass has grown,
A squirrel's dance, all on its own.
He scurries left, then darts to right,
Chasing shadows, what a sight!

Behind the bushes, tales unfold,
Of wandering shoes and secrets bold.
A lost umbrella claims its throne,
Next to a cactus, all alone.

Bicycles trapped in weeds so thick,
Shattered dreams of a childhood trick.
We find a treasure, winding paths,
Where laughter echoes, and joy lasts.

Chasing rabbits, hiding from the breeze,
Finding old socks among the trees.
In laughter's grip, we roam so free,
In hidden places, we should all be.

Tapestry of the Unseen

In the attic, dust bunnies thrive,
Old portraits whisper, 'We're alive!'
A forgotten trunk holds garish clothes,
Fashion failed, as everyone knows.

Beneath the floorboards, secrets dwell,
Of runaway socks, and a cat that fell.
A magic carpet that never flies,
Instead found under some garlic fries.

We weave a story from threads of cheer,
With mismatched socks, we conquer fear.
A playful yarn, our minds entwined,
In crafting chuckles, we're redefined.

From quirky patterns, we all spin,
Laughter's color bursts from within.
In unseen corners, joy is sewn,
A tapestry of fun we've grown.

Beneath the Canopy of Time

Amidst the trees, a picnic spread,
With ants debating on who gets bread.
A squirrel steals the last bite away,
And giggles echo through the day.

Time's canopy shields the silly fun,
With laughter bubbled like a run.
Chasing shadows in the fading light,
From behind the trunk, a playful fright.

Old watches ticking, but we stand still,
Catching moments like butterflies in thrill.
In our laughter, time takes a break,
As the wind whispers, "Make no mistake!"

Beneath layers of joy we find,
Life's little quirks, intricately signed.
So let's wander where giggles rhyme,
Beneath the branches, lost in time.

Blooms from Dusty Memories

In a garden where the weeds grow tall,
We unearth stories, big and small.
A gnome who's lost his pointy hat,
Sits amusingly next to a stately cat.

Petunias dressed in a polka-dot dress,
Whisper secrets with charming finesse.
A long-forgotten cake, now just crumbs,
With bees enjoying the sweet of their sums.

Beneath the sun where laughter sprouts,
Old toys gathered in well-loved bouts.
A rubber duck, yellow, quite out of place,
Grinning wide in the dusty space.

From scattered memories, blooms arrive,
Springing forth where old pranks thrive.
In this quirky garden, joy ignites,
With every chuckle, the past delights.

Resilience in the Unknown

In a garden full of laughter,
We grow despite the weather,
Dancing while the storm clouds gather,
Sipping tea with silly heather.

Wiggly worms in hats we wear,
Chasing shadows, unaware,
The daffodils start to sing,
As we jump and do our thing!

Every tree has silly dreams,
Dancing in the moonlit beams,
Branches twist and roots can grin,
Turns out weeds are all our kin!

With every wobble, laugh, and cheer,
Life's a circus, never fear,
We may stumble, yet we rise,
With goofy grins and bright blue skies!

Beneath the Surface

Swim inside the pond of glee,
Where giggles bubble silently,
Frogs wear crowns and splish-splash round,
In a world where fun is found.

We dig down low to find a prize,
A treasure chest with candy pies,
Silly moles with funny thinks,
They knit toques with fuzzy links!

Underneath, the secrets flow,
As the sun begins to glow,
Bubbling laughter fills the air,
While the squirrels gather to share!

Let's dive deep, embrace the swirl,
As magic spins and giggles whirl,
Life's a frolic, no doubt, son,
With a splash, we have our fun!

Whispers of the Earth

The ground beneath my pogo stick,
Whispers secrets, quick and slick,
Bouncing on the funky grass,
Every leap, a giggle blast!

Pigeons gossip with the breeze,
Tickling leaves on ancient trees,
"Hey, I saw a squirrel today!"
And we laugh as they all play.

Rocks will chuckle, stones will wink,
Palm trees sway and then they blink,
Nature's voice is sweetly bold,
Sharing stories yet untold!

Dancing roots beneath our feet,
Find a way to skip and meet,
With every chuckle, every cheer,
We hear the Earth, it whispers clear!

Ties That Bind

Through tangled vines and laughter loud,
We stumble 'neath the silly cloud,
Frogs in flip-flops start to dance,
As we twirl in fun romance!

Knitted scarves of leaves we wear,
Tangled mess in morning air,
A playful knot, we tie it tight,
With laughter, we take flight!

The world is full of silly strings,
Linked together, joy it brings,
We pull, we tug, we hop along,
Singing out a crazy song!

So let's connect and take a chance,
With giggles, twists, and goofy stance,
Each silly bond is full of cheer,
Together we'll conquer the year!

Sprouts of the Past

In the garden, ghosts of me,
Playing hide-and-seek with glee.
Tomatoes tell tales, oh so wild,
Of my antics as a careless child.

Carrots chuckle, wiggles and bends,
As I fight weeds, my unwelcome friends.
Lettuce whispers, 'Can't you see?',
Your childhood's sowed in dirt like me!'

The Colors of Connection

A blue potato pranced around,
While orange carrots danced on the ground.
Beets blushed red, all dressed to impress,
In the veggie ball, they caused quite a mess!

Zucchini jokes, never too stale,
Spilling the beans, or was it a kale?
Friendship blooms where sunlight streams,
In a patch of laughter, we chase our dreams.

Seeds of Solitude

I planted a seed, oh dear what a blunder,
It sprouted a smile, not just this and that under.
Cucumbers curled in their loner retreat,
Making plans to have a quiet meet.

A sunflower sighed, 'Leave me be,
I'm here for the shade, not company!'
Yet as they grew, they couldn't ignore,
How fun it is to be alone—and more!

Cradled by Earth

Down in the soil, things start to shift,
An earthworm's twitch can be quite the gift.
'Hey, look!' shouts a tiny pea pod,
'We're all just friends in this soggy clod!'

A cabbage complained in a leafy frown,
'I need a vacation, away from this town!'
Yet as roots mingle beneath the ground,
They laugh and they giggle, together they're found.

Hearth of the Heart

In caves of the couch, we find great cheer,
With snacks piled high and laughter near.
The cat claims the throne, a furry disgrace,
While we pretend it's our rightful place.

The fridge hums a tune, a melody sweet,
It calls to the hungry, can't accept defeat.
With leftovers dancing, a culinary show,
Who said that the kitchen can't steal the glow?

Old socks on the floor, my socks' secret fate,
Declare themselves treasures, consider it fate.
Together we'll giggle, through thick and thin,
For joy lives here even where dust bunnies spin.

Branching Out

I planted a dream, it grew like a weed,
With neighbors shaking heads, planting doubt's seed.
"Why not just garden?" they say with a sigh,
I'm planting a joke — give it time, let it fly!

Those branches are twisted, like stories untold,
Yet each one is shining, more precious than gold.
With fruit made of laughter, we pick every day,
In the orchard of folly, come join in the play.

We swing from our branches, precariously high,
Like acrobats bold, in the bright open sky.
As leaves shake with giggles, the sun starts to beam,
In this playground of whimsy, we chase every dream!

The Ties That Sustain

With noodle-like noodles, we weave through our days,
Each twist and each turn makes a marvelous maze.
A spaghetti connection, quite tangled and bright,
Together we slurp through the long, starry night.

The fabric of chaos, our cloak of delight,
With threads of mischief and laughter in flight.
We patch up our problems with quirky designs,
In this loony patchwork, hilarity shines.

So let's gather the yarns, through giggles abound,
We'll quilt up our mishaps with glee as the sound.
For in these weird stitches, we find what's aligned,
With hearts tied together, a gift that's refined!

The Loom of Existence

In the grand tapestry, absurdity spins,
With colors of chaos, where laughter begins.
Each thread holds a tale, woven with glee,
As I trip over socks and my cat laughs at me.

We tie up the stories, in knots of delight,
With patterns of mayhem, our future looks bright.
An apron of stories, we wear with a shrug,
While dancing on wobbles, we squish out a hug.

Each moment a fiber, a mischievous stitch,
Our loom hums a tune, both funny and rich.
In the workshop of giggles, where shenanigans blend,
We craft our existence, with no need to pretend!

The Pulse of Heritage

In grandma's garden, so much to see,
Tomatoes dance, and beans feel free.
A chicken struts with a snappy wig,
While a gopher plots, planning a dig.

Neighbors exchange their wild tales loud,
Of great Aunt Gertrude, the elephant crowd.
Laughter erupts, an uproarous cheer,
As ancient secrets become crystal clear.

Every recipe, a treasure chest,
Spices and stories, they truly zest!
The rhythm of life, a comical tune,
Where humor and history find room to bloom.

With salsa steps on a Sunday night,
And uncles who argue with all their might.
Traditions frolic, they jump and spin,
In this family circus, everyone wins!

Interwoven Histories

A tapestry woven with wild threads,
From uncles who bake, to aunts who wed.
Patterns of laughter, stitched with a grin,
And cousin Billy's mustache, a win.

History's tangled, but so much fun,
A picnic of stories under the sun.
Grandpa's tall tales stretch beyond the sky,
As everyone munches on homemade pie.

Uncle Joe's jokes, like tennis balls fly,
As friendly good-natured pranks pass by.
A family quilt, both quirky and bright,
Where every patch whispers tales of delight.

So let's raise a glass to the past we chew,
And the weird cousin who thinks he's a shrew.
With every stitch, the mirth intertwines,
In the crazy saga of our family lines.

The Terrain of Memory

Down memory lane, with a skip and a hop,
Where goofy mishaps never will stop.
Uncle Fred's hair looks like a bird's nest,
While Aunt Sue claims it's a fashion quest.

At picnics, the ants have their own parade,
While siblings argue about who's been played.
That old swing set, a throne for the brave,
Where laughter echoes, the footloose wave.

Mismatched socks worn by the family best,
Grandpa insists they wear 'em with zest.
Through gardens and fields, our tales take flight,
In the quirky quilt of our shared delight.

With ketchup fountains and ice cream fights,
Every grand story feels so just right.
In every moment, humor and tales,
In the landscape of laughter, our love prevails.

Treading the Familiar

In the old house where memories climb,
Every nook shares a silly rhyme.
Mom's cooking smells like a prankster's brew,
With garlic that's winking at Grandma too.

Stepping on toys is a rite of passage,
While family chaos is our shared message.
Dogs and cats take auditions for pets,
In this reality show of family bets.

Family games, with rules made up on the fly,
A hilarious mess that spirals on high.
We're comic book heroes in our own way,
With capes made from blankets, we save the day!

As we gather 'round, the stories rehash,
Of cousin Tim's beard, a laugh-filled splash.
So here's to our saga, a jolly parade,
In the dance of the familiar, we'll never fade.

Silent Connections

In the garden, gnomes all wink,
They gossip while I pour my drink.
Invisible ties, oh what a sight,
They chat and chuckle day and night.

The daisies dance, the weeds do sway,
They plot and scheme in a silly way.
One says, "Hey, let's hide the rake!"
Another laughs, "Oh what a prank to make!"

In the shadows, the spiders weave,
Their web of laughter, you won't believe.
They catch the sun and sparkle bright,
With jokes that tickle with pure delight.

So in the soil, mischief thrives,
With jokes exchanged, all nature jives.
In the quiet, connections bloom,
And laughter echoes through the room.

Tidal Roots

At the beach where sand meets sea,
Seagulls squawk in jubilee.
They dive for shrimp, they steal French fries,
It's a feast where humor lies.

The crabs do dance, they scuttle fast,
With sideways moves, they never last.
They poke and prod, then quickly flee,
Such agile jokers—they crack me!

The tide rolls in with a playful shove,
It splashes joy, a hand of love.
While seaweed wiggles, doing the twist,
I can't help but join in this tryst.

From clam to clam, the laughter flows,
As beachcombers share what each one knows.
With every wave, they find their fame,
In tidal whispers, all the same.

Canopy of Kinship

High above, the branches sway,
Birds gossip without delay.
They chirp of nuts and crumbs they've found,
While squirrels play—and tumble down!

The leaves all rustle, sharing news,
About the best and worst of views.
A raccoon sleeps through all the fun,
As shadows dance beneath the sun.

The sunlight filters through the green,
Where mischief lives, so pure, so keen.
Together, they craft a silly show,
In the canopy where laughter grows.

Branches knit like family ties,
Each gust of wind, a joyful surprise.
Swinging high, they cheer and play,
In their jolly, leafy ballet.

Notes from the Soil

The earth below, a chatterbox,
With worms that tickle 'round the rocks.
They send their quips from deep within,
Where all the giggles start to spin.

The ants march forth, they know their role,
With every crumb, they reach their goal.
Oh, how they laugh—as food they share,
A feast that makes all others stare!

A mole peeks up to join the jest,
He lifts a brow, feeling quite blessed.
With every poke, the soil erupts,
And nature's jokes are quite erupt!

So let us dig and take a chance,
Join in the fun, and laugh and dance.
For in the ground, surprises meet,
In every corner, life is sweet.

Wanderlust in the Soil

In the garden, gnomes take flight,
With their tiny backpacks, oh what a sight!
They travel the earth just like we do,
Chasing the sun and the morning dew.

The daisies dream of distant lands,
While worms write novels with their hands.
Bees buzzing tales of honeyed cheer,
While ants debate what's for lunch this year!

Above, the clouds are on a spree,
Dropping rain like confetti, oh me, oh my!
The mud puddles reflect the skies,
All while the frogs host a hopping surprise.

So when you dig deep, don't just despair,
You might unearth a party down there!
With nature's laughter and dirt on our shoes,
Let's take a tour of the world's buried views.

Tales of Unseen Connections

The broccoli's cousin claims to be wise,
Telling tales of the moonlit skies.
Carrots gossip in their cozy beds,
While the cabbage rolls its leafy heads.

An acorn dreams of a mighty oak,
While mushrooms share their fungi jokes.
The onions cry while they laugh in tears,
Slicing through the drama of vegetable fears.

Through tangled roots, friendships thrive,
As seedlings dance, oh they come alive!
Even weeds have stories, wild and free,
Plotting pranks on the honeybee.

So lend an ear to the ground below,
Where whispers of laughter and chaos flow.
Behind every sprout, there's mischief and glee,
In this hidden world, oh what a spree!

Echoes from the Earth

The gravel sings as we walk along,
Chirping out a gravelly song.
Rocks hold secrets of ages past,
While daisies chuckle, "This is a blast!"

Mountains beckon with big, bold grins,
While rivers laugh as the adventure begins.
Underneath, the roots do jig and whirl,
Pulling the ground in a whimsical twirl.

Mossy carpets hold stories untold,
Of weddings in whispers and treasures of old.
While snails, in tuxedos, glide down the path,
Singing sonnets in the aftermath.

So listen closely to the earth's own voice,
Every pebble and twig has made its choice.
In this living opera, we're all a part,
Echoes of nature, reaching the heart.

The Language of Old Trees

Beneath the bark, there's chatter galore,
Where the woodpeckers tap and the squirrels explore.
Old trees chuckle with branches outstretched,
Trading secrets that time has etched.

Their roots intertwine like old friends in chat,
Gossiping softly under a hat.
Fallen leaves share jokes on the ground,
While shadows dance as the breeze spins around.

The mighty oak tells tales of the nights,
When stars winked and the moon shared its lights.
Saplings lean in, wide-eyed and keen,
Listening close, caught in the scene.

So next time you wander, take a seat,
Among the giants, feel the heartbeat.
In their ancient laughter and wisdom, you'll see,
The forest is bursting with humor, oh gee!

Threads Woven through Time

In a garden of socks by the hedge,
Tangled tales of a time-travel pledge.
Grandpa's pants now a scarecrow's attire,
Fashion faux pas that just never tire.

Under the lawn where the daisies giggle,
Lies a net of yarn, oh so biggle!
Knitting the stories of yesteryears,
Even the cat seems to roll in cheers.

There's a scarf made from whispers and jokes,
A tapestry woven by quirky folks.
Every patch echoes a mischievous grin,
Socks in the corner, a soft winds' spin.

When the world spins round like a spinning top,
The threads come alive, they twist and hop.
Around the fire, they dance with delight,
Knitting up laughter all through the night.

Cradles of Forgotten Dreams

In a closet of shadows, secrets reside,
Old toys and wishes that once took a ride.
A bicycle rusts next to a teddy bear,
While dust bunnies plot like no one's aware.

Dreams float like balloons from a long-ago fair,
Juggling memories that dance in the air.
An old pair of boots with a whimsical knot,
Once ran through the rain. Now they laugh a lot!

The robot who dances with two left feet,
Still spins and twirls, a remarkable feat.
With a rusted hinge and a playful twang,
He's the king of the cradles, where dreams still hang.

In the attic of giggles, where time plays the tune,
A chorus of whispers beneath the moon.
Each cradle a melody of childhood's gems,
Replaying the laughter, forever it stems.

Nature's Embrace

Beneath the oak, where the squirrels pray,
A sandwich picnic turns nature's play.
Ants march in rows like they own the place,
While dandelions smile, their fluffy lace.

The river chuckles with a bubbly cheer,
Sipping on dreams and a cold lemonade here.
While frogs in tuxedos sing karaoke,
And the dragonflies buzz a sweet little homily.

In the meadow, where the daisies debate,
Butterflies gossip, it's quite the fate.
Each breeze carries giggles and tickling leaves,
As nature unfolds its fantastic sleeves.

With roots and shoots in a silly dance,
The world spins round, oh, let's take a chance!
To dive in the mud and make a grand splash,
In nature's embrace, we giggle and dash!

Whispers Beneath the Surface

The pond holds secrets in ripples so sly,
Frogs croak conspiracies with every sigh.
Fish wear tiaras, and ducks strut about,
Hosting a soirée where nobody shouts.

Beneath the waves, all the chatter abounds,
Bubbles exchange gossip and silly sounds.
A sunken shoe tells tales of last summer,
While turtles share stories, all in a hummer.

An octopus joins in with a wink and a nod,
Juggling the seaweed and giving a prod.
His eight arms waving like they're in a band,
Performing the waltz for the sea's merry land.

As laughter rises, floaters join in spree,
Underwater whimsy, oh, what a sight to see!
With whispers unleashed in a splash of delight,
The pond's cheerful secrets dance day and night.

Nature's Embrace

In the garden, worms parade,
Dancing to a soil-made jingle,
Rabbits hop, a grand charade,
While squirrels plot a nutty mingle.

Bees wear hats of pollen gold,
Buzzing tales of flowery cheer,
Trees gossip, their branches bold,
"Did you see that bee over here?"

Ducks discuss the weather's rise,
Quacking jokes that waddle far,
While frogs croak 'neath starlit skies,
Hoping for a swampy bazaar.

Leaves crackle in a happy dance,
The sun tickles blades with beams,
Nature knows how to take a chance,
And giggles in our wildest dreams.

Connection's Canvas

On the porch, a cat and dog,
Side by side, they share a snooze,
They dream of birds, and chase a fog,
Who knew, they'd form this quirky goo?

Pigeons gossip on the line,
"Have you seen that human fall?"
While the squirrels claim it's divine,
To raid the feeder and the call.

Grasshoppers play a lively tune,
Jumping high with a leafish cheer,
While ants march, neat as a boon,
In formation, bold and sincere.

In every garden, life connects,
With laughter stitched in every seam,
Nature's humor, what it affects,
A canvas bright, a playful dream.

The Flutter of Wings

In the park, a pigeon struts,
With swagger and a quite loud coo,
While butterflies in frilly cuts,
Whirl in skirts of vibrant hue.

Bees play tag with buzzing zest,
Flitting fast from bloom to bloom,
They claim that they are the best,
In the contest of sweet perfume.

A heron tries to do ballet,
In shallow ponds, it takes a stand,
With a splash, it turns to say,
"I'm graceful, just like you planned!"

Nests are built with funny flair,
Twigs and trash, all in a heap,
Nature's art is everywhere,
With every wing, a giggle leap.

Hidden Histories

In the attic, treasures hide,
Old shoes that once went on a trip,
A teddy bear, the tears he dried,
Mysteries in every zip.

Family photos tell a tale,
Of hairstyles lost, and eyeglasses slid,
Uncle Bob, in neon veil,
Dancing like he just got rid.

Grandma's letters, faded proof,
Of love that wrapped like warmest pies,
In every crest, a hidden truth,
Of giggles whispered 'neath the skies.

Those who've left behind a trace,
In dusty boxes, laughter swells,
Life's funny in its winding race,
With stories sweet, like secret shells.

The Dark Green Veil

In the garden, plants conspire,
Wearing hats made from old wire.
They gossip about growing tall,
While squirrels sneak and make a haul.

The weeds wear crowns, they think they're grand,
Throwing shade on the flower stand.
A sunflower winks, says, 'How's it fair?'
While tulips dance without a care.

Among the leaves, a spider spins,
Telling tales where mischief begins.
With every breeze, a chuckle flows,
As garden gnomes swap silly clothes.

Laughter blooms by everyday toil,
As earthworms plot in cozy soil.
In this patch, a secret unfolds,
Where nature wears its antics bold.

The Lifeblood of Place

In the café, the coffee's high,
While cakes jump 'round and say, 'Oh my!'
The barista, juggling cups with flair,
Makes us wonder, 'How's he up there?'

Behind the counter, a dog named Lou,
Serves biscuits, think he's quite the brew!
With wagging tail, he steals the show,
As patrons giggle, 'He's the pro!'

The tables play a game of charades,
As chairs whisper of old escapades.
Every sip's a note in the tune,
While spoons dance beneath the afternoon.

In this corner of laughter and cream,
People bond over the silliest dream.
The lifeblood flows with joy and grace,
Creating a home in that lively space.

Circles of Wisdom

In the park, a bench is wise,
Where pigeons meet to share their lies.
They gossip 'bout the humans they find,
And laugh at the joggers, oh so blind!

The trees raise brows, in silent jokes,
While crickets chirp, like playful blokes.
One leaf says, 'I'm the wisest here,'
While daisies giggle, 'Oh, my dear!'

An old oak grumbles, 'Wait your turn,'
Circling stories where branches churn.
Each ring tells tales of days gone by,
While squirrels plot how to touch the sky.

Underfoot, the grasses hum a tune,
As shadows stretch beneath the moon.
In circles gathered, wisdom's shared,
With every secret that nature dared.

Tides of Belonging

At the beach, the waves do prance,
With sandcastles giving it a chance.
Seagulls squawk, but they're out of tune,
Trying to dance to a playful tune.

The tide rolls in, takes shells for a ride,
While children giggle, with joy they glide.
As crabs play tag and flip in the foam,
The ocean whispers, 'Welcome home!'

Banners of seaweed wave in delight,
While flip-flops scatter, taking flight.
Every splash is a burst of cheer,
In the ebb and flow, all feel near.

With laughter tugging at the shore,
Each wave brings friends and so much more.
In this tide of fun, we all belong,
As nature sings its joyful song.

The Unsung Bonds

In the attic, a trunk sat still,
Full of memories, laughs, and a thrill.
A cousin's sock from sixty-one,
Promises kept, but who's got the fun?

Last Thanksgiving, a turkey fell,
A family brawl with a pot's loud yell.
Great Aunt Mabel found in a hat,
The secret sauce for a thousand chats!

Silly photos, each face a tease,
Uncle Bob dances with jelly under his knees.
Every moment stitched in time's embrace,
The craziest ties, you wouldn't trade for a race.

So here's to love in every range,
Laughter, like ketchup, gets all the strange.
From closets wide to corners dark,
They're our family, they leave a mark!

Footprints Forgotten

In my garden, a shoe's long lost,
Probably left when the game went tossed.
Bouncing balls, laughter in the sun,
Where'd it go? Oh, the search isn't fun!

An uncle's tale of a pie-thief glare,
A squirrel claimed it; oh, life's unfair!
Chasing shadows of sneakers gone,
Waiting for rain while I'm stuck in a con.

Each step tells stories of mischief in grass,
Like stepping on gum or falling with sass.
The garden is wild, the world quite daft,
But memories linger, forever a laugh.

So here's to the paths we grin and stomp,
With a giggle and cheer, let's all just romp.
For every lost shoe, a tale to share,
Like my Uncle's hat that just vanished in air!

The Limbs of Time

A tree sat crooked, its branches askew,
Hats on the leaves, 'What's a tree to do?'
With squirrels debating who gets the prime seat,
While ants have a rave at its roots' cozy meet.

Each limb tells a story of weathered cheer,
Of picnics with pie and a buzzing bee's leer.
Grandma's apron caught in a playful breeze,
Now a dandelion's hat, oh, who's got the keys?

The knots in the bark hold secrets we share,
Like little whispers, "Remember that flare?"
Time may twist us into tales of jest,
But each quirky limb knows we're truly blessed.

So, let's gather round for tales and glee,
Watch out for squirrels; they're crafty, you see!
From branches to roots, let laughter unfurl,
In the dance of a tree, there's magic to twirl!

Intertwined Journey

Two paths crossed with giggles and glares,
One was lost, but the other just dares.
Wobbly wheelbarrows, a clumsy old race,
With mud on our faces, joy lit up the place.

Through puddles and thickets, we ran like wild,
Each fall a victory, oh, we were styled!
A stick as a sword, a crown made of twigs,
Knights of the garden, with frogs as our digs.

Every turn a tale of laughter and mess,
With encounters of ants and that one big stress.
But no matter the mishaps, we danced through the day,
With friendships entwined like a grand cabaret.

So here's to the journey, both silly and bright,
With fun at each corner, all wrongs turned to right.
Grab hands, let's giggle as we spin into fate,
For the best of our tales are ones we create!

Forest of Familiarity

In a wood where laughter grows bright,
The squirrels tell jokes, what a sight!
Trees gossip about the old days,
While branches shake in funny ways.

Mushrooms dance like a wobbly band,
Fungi in hats, isn't that grand?
Bugs have parties, they break out in cheer,
Who knew plants had a sense of jeer!

Acorns wearing bow ties quite neat,
Oh look, there's a snail on a beet!
Wind whispers secrets in charm,
The forest is full of delightful harm.

In this grove, the laughter never ends,
Familiar faces, and some odd friends.
Rules of nature, twisted with fun,
In this land, we're all number one!

Bonds that Thrive

Two plants argue, who's taller for sure?
The daisies giggle; they can't take the lure!
The vines intertwine, in a silly embrace,
A snail on a leaf, now that's quite the race!

In every garden, there's punchlines galore,
Rabbits joke, 'We can't take any more!'
The flowers are busy gossiping loud,
While bees buzz around, feeling quite proud.

A worm in a hat gives a wink from the soil,
Says, 'Life's just a party, let's dance and uncoil!'
Petunias chuckle, their petals all bright,
In this colorful world, everything's right!

Friendship blooms in the garden of cheer,
With laughter and smiles from ear to ear.
So here's to the bonds that make us all thrive,
With humor and joy, we truly arrive!

Currents of Unity

In a stream so lively, fish swim and sway,
Splashing with giggles in a water ballet.
Turtles bobbing, trying to float,
While ducks quack jokes; oh, what a gloat!

The reeds are swaying, they join in the fun,
Each wave brings laughter, they dance, they run.
Frogs leap along, in a grand old spree,
Croaking the chorus of unity!

The sun shines bright, it can't help but grin,
Even the rocks are drawn in the din.
They chuckle together, quite polished and sly,
As the river rolls on, 'Oh me, oh my!'

Together they flow, in a jolly parade,
Every splash promising joy will cascade.
Celebrating their quirks, they share one refrain,
In the currents of friendship, there's never disdain!

The Language of Earth

In fields of chatter where daisies hum,
The grass gets tickled, 'Oh, isn't it fun?'
Clovers debate which one's the luckiest,
While ladybugs laugh at who's the funniest!

The earthworm writes poems deep underground,
Telling jokes only he has found.
The beetles applaud, 'That's a good one, mate!'
Caterpillars roll, saying, 'We can't wait!'

The rocks sit still, but their laughter's deep,
Whispering sounds in a way that we leap.
The mud makes puns, squelching with glee,
'Life's like a party; come dance with me!'

In this patch of giggles, it's hard to resist,
Nature's own humor, a twist on the mist.
So join in the fun, under sun, rain, and mirth,
In the great big playground — the language of Earth!

Fragments of Shared Existence

In the garden of life, quite a sight,
Nuts and bolts dance under the moonlight.
Whispers of laughter, in shadows they creep,
Finding lost socks in the soil so deep.

A carrot named Carl with a top hat so grand,
Tells tales of his brothers from the neighboring land.
Potatoes argue about who's the best,
While the eggs take a nap, they need their rest.

The chives have a gossip, what's hot on the grill,
As pickles and onions hatch plans for a thrill.
In the whirl of the veggies, they celebrate fate,
Who knew salad could host such a fun state?

So hand me a plate, let's feast with delight,
As roots intertwine in this wild agrarian fight.
Fragments of life, together they dance,
Enjoying the chaos, just give it a chance.

The Bloodline of the Landscape

In the dust of the fields, the gossip flies,
Chickens spouting news with their beady eyes.
The sunflowers nod as they sway to the beat,
While carrots discuss the latest street meet.

A cantaloupe king on his fruity throne,
Claims he's the juiciest, oh how he's grown!
The radishes snicker, they know there's no doubt,
They're crunchier, brighter, and never pass out.

The pumpkins roll dice under stars bright and bold,
Arguing about who is the greatest of old.
A wave from the corn, in rows like a crowd,
Cheering on tales that are funny and loud.

As nighttime descends, the critters convene,
To plot out adventures, both wild and unseen.
Each plant shares a story, a twist or a jest,
In the bloodline of landscape, they pass every test.

Echoes of the Ancients

Old trees tell stories with their creaky groans,
While squirrels exchange tales in muffled tones.
The mushrooms are busy, with ear to the ground,
Eavesdropping secrets where laughter is found.

A wise old oak boasts of a time long past,
When ants wrote the scripts, and the shadows cast.
Each bark has a wrinkle, a humorous twist,
Of critters with antics you simply can't miss.

The ancient stones chuckle, they've seen it all,
When nature's mistakes became quite the brawl.
Little beetles discussing their latest plight,
Chasing their dreams in the cool starry night.

With echoes that giggle, the world spins around,
These ancient vibrations harmonize sound.
From roots deep below to the skies up above,
In every wise whisper, there's laughter and love.

Waking the Silent Earth

As dawn gently tickles the sleeping old ground,
A worm stirs awake, with his body unwound.
He stretches quite wide, gives a yawn, then he grins,
Saying, "Time to dig in, let the fun begin!"

The ants march like soldiers, all snazzy and neat,
In their tiny brigade, they've got lunch to greet.
A beetle on wheels zooms by with a laugh,
While the grass sprinkles dew like a joyful photograph.

The daisies all gossip, "Did you hear what was said?"
As they spice up their plots about how to be fed.
While rocks chat excitedly, they roll with a jig,
"Oh what a morning! Let's dance like a twig!"

In this waking of earth, life's vibrant and spry,
Every creature watching as the day passes by.
With humor and hustle, they burst into play,
To celebrate the gift of a brand new day.

Garden of Collective Memories

In the garden where we play,
Thoughts of gumdrops float away.
The daffodils dance, a cheeky crew,
They giggle and wink at the morning dew.

A tree with glasses reads a book,
A fruit bat stirs with a funny look.
Squirrels trade secrets, wearing tiny hats,
While rabbits join in with their acrobat chats.

The fence is painted with tales untold,
Of summer feats and braves so bold.
Each flower, a story that tickles the mind,
In this quirky plot where laughter's entwined.

When the sun dips low and shadows loom,
We laugh at the shadows that start to bloom.
Memories sprout from the silliest seeds,
In this garden where giggles exceed our needs.

The Heartbeat of the Unfolding

Tick-tock goes the clock on the wall,
As socks march in line - oh, what a haul!
From kitchen to garden, they trip on the ground,
With a rhythm so funny, it's joy that we've found.

The daisies hum tunes to the beat of a drum,
While ants do the cha-cha - oh, what's to come?
With each plant that's sprouting, a giggle takes wing,
As nature's chorus prepares to sing.

Birds in a frenzy, they're planning a show,
A dance-off in sunlight, all set to go.
The daisies are judges, holding tiny signs,
While worms wiggle low in their sparkly lines.

With every tick of the timepiece so bold,
There's humor in nature, its stories unfold.
And we sway with the breeze, in this wild jubilee,
Laughing at life, just being carefree.

Homecoming to Forgotten Places

Off we go to places once neat,
Where dust bunnies tango and old shoes retreat.
Ancient chairs that creak like a jazz band,
And pizza boxes stacked like a tall, funny stand.

The fridge with its secrets, it gives us a wink,
A leftover mystery, what do you think?
While curtains have stories of laughter and tears,
In corners where echo our childhood years.

We tiptoe through memories hidden in stacks,
Tripping on treasures and dusty knickknacks.
It's here that the oddities gleefully bloom,
In this quirky old place, we shake off the gloom.

With each silly laugh shared, the past comes alive,
In forgotten areas where whimsies thrive.
Homecoming's a dance, with friends all around,
In places where joy's forever unbound.

The Symphony of Seasons Past

Frogs in tuxedos croak out a tune,
In marshmallow clouds, under the moon.
The leaves tap their feet, with colors so bright,
As we dance with the seasons, what a silly sight!

The winter flakes swirl like dancers in lace,
While snowmen chuckle, sprouting a face.
Springtime arrives with a hop and a shake,
As flowers join in, for goodness' sake!

Summer's a party, with sun hats galore,
As fruits juggle names that keep us in store.
Fall throws confetti in colors so bold,
With pumpkins that giggle at stories retold.

The symphony plays with a whimsical cheer,
As time does a twirl, and memories steer.
In the dance of the seasons, we giggle away,
Crafting moments that brighten our day.

Traces of Belonging

In every nook, a story hides,
A sock from Auntie, a bear that glides.
Grandpa's tales of fish so grand,
Turned out to be just loose rubber bands.

Cousins gather with quirk on display,
One thinks pie is proper ballet.
Aunt May, confused, brings casserole shaped,
Like a cat that the dog once draped.

Chairs creak under laughter's weight,
We trip on jokes, it's never too late.
Jokes told in whispers, laughter in flight,
Echoes of joy on a quiet night.

With every bite, old flavors collide,
Spinach pie? Oh, please, not my pride!
Yet there in the pantry, love's ample store,
We feast on fun, and always want more.

The Hidden Tapestry

Woven with threads from the strangest themes,
A quilt made of dad's old ripped-up jeans.
Mom stitched a patch with cats on the prowl,
While Uncle Bob yells, 'Where's my towel?'

Each stitch a mishap, a humorous claim,
The ironing? One big, fun game!
A dog ran through, left a scruffy trace,
Now it's front and center, this weaving disgrace!

The grand reveal is met with a cheer,
'This is art, we all hold dear!'
But still it looks like a fabric fight,
Like socks after laundry, oh what a sight!

Gather 'round to admire the flair,
We share in giggles while fixing the tear.
Though threads may unravel, love's never far,
It's cozy and funny; that's who we are.

Echoes of Ancestry

An old photo hangs, faces all bunched,
Great-great-grandma, with hair that's crunched.
She's holding a pickle, the size of her head,
We ask who in this clan drank pickle juice red?

Uncle Joe claims it's proof he's the best,
At chugging down pickles, forget all the rest!
We laugh as we ponder the legends of yore,
Of daring dares, and so much more.

With every strange name, a chuckle awakes,
Ethel Too-Sassy, and then Gus with the cakes.
An echo of laughter, a family blend,
In the book of our kin, the fun has no end!

We toast to the quirks, the oddities shared,
For every goof up, someone prepared.
With tales that waddle and wobble just right,
Ancestral laughter lights up the night.

Scattered Seeds

Little seeds of laughter, tossed far and wide,
Sprouting wild stories we cannot abide.
One grew a mustache on a scarecrow's face,
While another danced off to a distant place.

Peppery anecdotes, each thorn and each bloom,
Craft prankish fables that lighten the room.
Around every corner, a giggle takes root,
As we share our mishaps in skipping the flute.

In the garden of jokes where silliness thrives,
We stumble on punchlines as each one arrives.
With blossoms of giggles waving up high,
The harvest of humor, our favorite pie.

So plant a few dreams, and watch them take flight,
In this bonkers patch where the sun shines bright.
For laughter's the bloom that can heal any bruise,
Scattered and wild, it's the best kind of muse.

Echoes from the Ground

In the garden, weeds dance around,
Snakes wearing hats, what a sight found!
Bunnies are laughing, in a two-step groove,
Who says the soil can't make you move?

The sprout in the pot thinks it's a queen,
Waving at ants who are bustling unseen.
A squirrel spins tales, quite full of cheer,
While pondering why nutty dreams disappear!

The daisies gossip, whispering quick
About the shy roots that play hide-and-seek.
The ground below hums a silly tune,
As earthworms wiggle beneath the full moon!

In this crazy garden, full of delight,
Each critter has stories that simply ignite.
With laughter erupting from every crevice,
Oh, what a grand place to chuckle and relish!

Patterns of Existence

In the kitchen, a dance of spoons and forks,
As I stir the pot, spaghetti walks and talks.
Tomato sauce giggles, what a big mess,
Trying to impress the old garlic press!

Under the fridge, the dust bunnies roam,
Gathering gossip about who's made it home.
The blender sings loudly, quite out of tune,
As veggies complain they miss the moon!

The fridge hums a tune, oh so sweet,
While leftovers plot to escape on their feet.
A plate of old eggs, not too keen to part,
They're forming a band with a youthful tart!

In this mad kitchen, the laughter erupts,
With spatulas dancing and no one interrupts.
Mixing the chaos, a humorous quest,
Every meal served is a funny fest!

Connected by Chronicles

There's a tree in the park, not so tall,
Telling secrets of squirrels in a ball.
Leaves gossip loudly, like brave little spies,
As branches reach out, conspiring with skies.

The benches are chairs for the gossipers' crowd,
With petals and bees buzzing life out loud.
A dog in sunglasses, quite suave in his walk,
Scribbles love letters that make the trees squawk!

The ducks in the pond, such philosophers wise,
Debating the merits of twinkling night skies.
Their quacks, a symphony of life's little jokes,
While turtles sit back, enjoying the pokes!

Together they weave the tales that they share,
With nature's orchestra playing everywhere.
In this patch of laughter, where joy does reside,
Every creature's story, impossibly wide!

The Map of My Heart

My heart's a map drawn in whimsical art,
With spots marked for laughter, a treasure to start.
A dotted line leads to giggles that glow,
While rivers run deep with the funny we know.

X marks the place where the hiccup sprouted,
While gags and puns, it lovingly touted.
The mountains are jokes that rise up so high,
And valleys of laughter where dreams soar and fly.

Every twist and turn, a story unfolds,
Of silly mishaps that never grow old.
The compass spins wildly, can't find north true,
Yet all that I seek is the joy shared with you!

With each beat, my map whirls and sighs,
A journey of fun wrapped in sweet surprise.
So let's trace the lines where the chuckles will start,
For wherever we wander, we'll dance heart to heart!

Stories of the Soil

In a garden where daisies play,
Worms throw parties every day.
Caterpillars dance in the sun,
Sipping nectar, oh what fun!

The radishes gossip, it's quite a scene,
About the carrots and their sheen.
Tomatoes blush with sweet delight,
While peas argue who's the best at flight.

Underneath, a creature's tale,
A mole who dreams of grander trails.
With funny hats and tiny shoes,
He whispers secrets to the snoozing snooze.

So when you dig beneath that mound,
You'll find friends dancing all around.
In every nook, a laugh does sprout,
In soil's embrace, there's joy about!

The Heartbeat of Land

The soil hums a quirky tune,
As ants march under the bright blue moon.
Chickens cluck in a punchy beat,
While moles tap dance with tiny feet.

Dandelions hold a comedy show,
With bees laughing at their flow.
The grass sways, in rhythm they sway,
As rocks tell stories of yesterday.

The trees chuckle in the breeze,
Their leaves understand life's little tease.
A squirrel narrates with flair and pride,
While butterflies giggle and glide.

Each corner shares a funny jest,
In land's embrace, we're all blessed.
With every heartbeat, stories unfold,
A banquet of laughter that never gets old!

The Soul's Understory

Underneath where shadows creep,
The mushrooms hold their laughter deep.
Fungi in hats toast with cheer,
While crickets serenade the ear.

A vine tickles a sleeping leaf,
Causing giggles, oh what a brief!
In a world where veggies jest,
They're having fun, you can't contest.

Rabbits share their carrot cakes,
While owls debate on quirky fakes.
A badger reading a funny book,
In the forest's heart, take a look.

Life beneath is glorious and free,
A boisterous choir, a place to be.
In this jungle of playful minds,
The soul enjoys what laughter finds!

Hidden Kinfolk

In every patch where tall grass tilts,
A family of crickets hums and wilts.
Their jokes echo through the field,
In joy, their happy hearts are sealed.

Under leaves, a raccoon peers,
Confused by the sound of merry cheers.
He joins in with a snicker, too,
Saying, "Why not?! I'll dance with you!"

The hedgehogs host a cozy feast,
With snacks that make the laughter beast.
While foxes tell of silly pranks,
And everyone chuckles, giving thanks.

So when you wander past the trees,
Look closely—find the family bees.
In every burrow, in every nook,
You'll find kinfolk, it's a funny book!

Veins of the Village

In every yard, a tale unfolds,
A chicken's dance, a story told.
The goats play tag, the pigs just snooze,
While Grandma knits, the village muse.

The postman's bike, a rattling show,
With letters tied, a jolly flow.
A cat on a fence, thinking it's grand,
Winks at the dog with a knowing hand.

Beneath old trees, the gossip spins,
Of who's had luck and who just grins.
Neighbors laugh, with joy in the air,
As silly hats are worn with flair.

The village grows, through thick and thin,
We're all just misfits with a grin.
Each corner shared, each laugh we glean,
In our funny world, it's a lively scene.

Flickers of Tradition

At Sunday feasts, we save the best,
Uncles dance, putting skills to test.
Auntie drops pies, oh what a sight,
While everyone cheers, 'Now that's polite!'

We twirl in suits, mismatched but proud,
As Grandma shouts, her voice so loud.
The secret recipe? You guessed it, spry!
Baking soda high—reach for the sky!

Games of charades, we're all confused,
Granddad's moves leave us bemused.
He mimics a cow, a pirate with flair,
His hat's too small, just like his hair!

With each odd dance, our hearts collide,
In laughter and love, there's nowhere to hide.
Tradition's a laugh, a joyful bend,
In every flicker, our fun won't end.

Shadows of the Past

Old photos lie, the faces grin,
With wacky hair, and glasses thin.
Our family tree, a tangled maze,
With Uncle Joe in those wild days.

The tales they share, a mix of strange,
Of how they danced, oh what a change!
From disco vibes to a line or two,
We shake our heads, 'Did they really do?'

Grandma's old stories, a riot unmasked,
Of that one time, she dared them, unasked.
The time she tripped, on mom's big hat,
The laughter erupted, just like that!

In shadows we chuckle, as memories blast,
Each silly grin, ties us to the past.
We gather our quirks, make them a feast,
In the heart of the funny, we're always least.

Fragments of Home

Peeking through windows, what can be seen?
A frog on the porch, sitting so keen.
The toaster's on strike, making a stand,
While dishes are piled up high—oh, so grand!

With socks on the line, chaos at play,
A paper boat floats, in the rain's ballet.
Each creaky board sings its old tune,
While we serenade the afternoon moon.

The kitchen's a hub, cooking mishaps galore,
Where soup gets too salty and naps become war.
Dad's secret stash of chocolate bites,
Are the currency for late-night delights.

Fragments collected, our laughter does bloom,
In wild little quirks, we dance in our room.
A mishmash of chaos, yet it feels right,
In our funny home, every day's a delight.

www.ingramcontent.com/pod-product-compliance
Lightning Source LLC
Chambersburg PA
CBHW070317120526
44590CB00017B/2716